A collection of stories written by silly old me, a bucks
know, this book took me nearly half a dozen crayons
however, it does include stories of a soldier's daily inte
the prospect of it can't get any fucking worse than this
you laugh and anyone who has served can relate to.

The story of FYB

Before Fill Your Boots, there was Gopping Berets, before that, there was The Tom's Liberation Front.

Who is behind these pages? Who is the admin behind the curtain? Well some would describe him as an extremely handsome, well rounded individual, whose only problem in life is getting too much arse.

He sashays around all day in his dressing gown, drinking Corona, only getting dressed to leave the house in order to take photos of hats in kit in the local supermarket. He claims back tax for a living although you'd never know this as he rarely speaks about it.

While still in, serving out his promotion bans like a champ, he decided social media was the way to go when he was getting out. Knowing his only qualifications were his ability to absolutely own people in the comments on FB he decided to trial it as a full-time job.

Running FYB while serving was a very tricky thing to handle. Much like Batman, by day he would be a completely straight bloke, getting shit done. But at night, at night he would turn into an online Troll to deal blows to the rancid hats he saw before him. Based in Colchester he was blessed with an abundance of photo opportunities including some of the biggest screamers known to man.

Having signed off he went into cruise mode, ironically, and no word of a lie, he was given a role in the Int cell to smash blokes on PERSEC. In short, the Army was now paying for him to catfish blokes and then give briefs at company / battalion levels about what not to give away online.

This was a sweet gig, and it was amazing that any Reg blokes would class this as "work", it was a true moment of inspiration and these craphats were great source material for the starting of FYB.

FYB, how did it get so big?

This was the time when the FYB page had 100s not 1ks or 10ks of followers. He needed something big for it to rocket and go viral.

This "something big" was still needed, and it came in the shape of the RMP. They delivered what he deemed to be the greatest WAH in the history of the Military. Whilst still serving, the comedy genius posted a link on FYB saying a certain bloke had tried to sleep with his missus and they would be named and shamed. The link was a prank as everyone who clicked on it would simply be directed to their own Facebook timeline. Whilst some got no more than a wry smile out of it, the mongs out there would believe that they had been named and shamed, and then the fun started…

A short while after posting this blatant bite he received a call from an RMP Cpl based in Colchester, the poor little poppet said if his profile was not removed from the page he would press charges (although what charges he would face were never mentioned). There was a denial about posting his profile and this correspondence went around in circles for a little while, ending with the irate RMP warning Mr FYB to "stand by", he then hung up. I'm not going to lie; I was giddy with excitement.

We fast forward this sorry tale to a sunny sports afternoon; whilst sitting in the top corridor office the previous mentioned Cpl arrives, accompanied by his Captain. The officer was snapping, frothing at the mouth, indignant with rage and started belt feeding 100 questions. What evidence was there that this poor Cpl was being so unceremoniously outed as a snake of the highest order. And the particularly brilliant "so you think you can post me and get away with it?".

It became obvious at this point, that while there were batteries in the monkey, its cymbal was not clanging.

Yes, the Cpl had gone to his boss with the issue of his impeachable character being slandered, The Captain had decided to see what the fuss was all about, clicked the link and saw his own profile. The penny failed to drop. He believed he'd also been posted…

Once again, the troll denied posting either of their profiles whilst also admitting he is the only admin of the group. Increasing in frustration and positively confused, the magician decided to reveal his secrets. "Sir, Cpl, it is simple, whoever clicks on the link will be taken to their own profile". This simple statement was met with the reply "Then why has no one else complained!?" With all the enthusiasm of someone who knows they have a mere three months left in the Military and all fucks he had been issued had been returned to stores he gleefully responded "maybe no one else is that much of a mong?"

After endless worry, the troll was told no further action would be taken… what nice guys.

Once freed of the shackles of Military life 18 hours a day was allocated to FYB, turning it into a small empire of 130 thousand likeminded souls all eager to uphold the values and standards of the Military by hammering any lizards found monging it. FYB quickly grew to become what many strongly believe to be the funniest, most informative and community based military publication of the digital age.

FYB may have been made by a cunt, but it's been shaped and built by a group of them. The Service and Veteran community.

Foreword

This a collection of thoughts and dits by a bloke. A bloke who wears a dressing gown and sells Avon, a bloke called Alfie Usher, KGB, AVON rep of the year and social alligator... Snap snap.

I have thought long and hard about how this book should be structured, how best to display my writing prowess if you will. I wanted to capture my innate ability of putting pen to paper. Then I remembered; I'm a complete mumbling mong, who for some reasons attracts mongs to a Facebook page to mock other mongs. You'll notice these aren't in any logical order, because that's nit #Armylogic.

Contents

To set the stall for this tale of adventure, let me introduce you to our main protagonist. Private Crowbag is in his early twenties and from Northern England, he joined an Infantry regiment due to his BARB and fitness test results. As a comparison, if you wanted to join the Pioneers and dig holes for a living, the BARB score is 40 out of 80, to join as an infantryman... it's 26. He is neither solid nor switched on, average fitness, and quite liked by his section. He is currently in week 14 out of 28 in training and is preparing for TAC EX 2.

It's Friday afternoon and Pte Crowbag has been stood down for the weekend to allow for vital preparation time ahead of his deployment on Tac Ex 2. It's a rude o'clock start on Monday morning so he really needs to follow the 7 P's of Prior Preparation and Planning will Prevent Piss Poor Performance. The staff have drilled him, briefed him, debriefed him and trained him for this moment, this is his time to shine.

It's at this point he notices that whilst the "straight blokes" start sorting their kit instantly and head off to pest at kit down the NAAFI and Drop Zone in town, the other end of the spectrum start gearing up for a weekend on the lash no doubt only to panic pack on a Sunday still doing their kit at 2 am on Monday morning, he is fully aware that these are also the idiots that will have no issues in waking up others asking if they have spare waterproof bags.

As we know, our hero is a taking being the grey man seriously and spends his weekend packing a little bit here and a little bit there with his kit fully squared for Sunday evening so he can rest up easy.

Monday morning, reveille and so it begins; shaved, world's fastest breakfast and block jobs all sorted before 7am. Pte Crowbag lines up with the rest of the platoon outside in the pissing rain for the dreaded kit checks. Having spent hours packing kit and individually waterproofing his socks he sees no benefit in unwrapping them to get them soaked in the rain, only to wrap them back up and put damp socks into his Bergan. It's that annoying amount of rain in Catterick, enough to get your stuff piss wet through but not hard enough that the depot staff think "fuck this" and shit can the inspection.

The kit inspection was a cluster, and his internal monologue narrated it as if David Attenborough himself was making the observations. The obvious displays are on show, oil bottles filled with half oil, half water, to make them appear full. Weapon cleaning kits are diffy everything but that sponge on a stick thing that no one can tell you what it's actually for and a combi-tool that was borrowed from someone else. The all-time classic spare waterproof bags, individually waterproofed of course, were resplendent in their singularly pointless existence. After a couple of laps around the blocks for someone else's mistakes, where it in no way paid to be a winner, Pte Crowbag now stuffs his now sodden kit back in his Bergen in a complete frenzy so it appears to be like he is man packing a fucking F-16. Now the call for moving out has come. Going for the lightning stripe Navy SEAL look, but ending more like he's blacked up, Pte Crowbag has got his cam cream out and tried his best to apply what most would describe as a tar like substance to his face, hands and neck. Application of which should be like pulling a NAAFI chick (easy) but for some reason feels more like passing a Brecon 2 miler as an RLC reservist (hard). He is all squared and getting ready to move off when some inept 2IC (who happens to be one of the retards who were on the piss all weekend) comes running over and chucks random shit for Pte Crowbag to carry. Stag shit, maps, pickaxe, fucking ECM if he had one, proper jacked on, but he bites the bullet and packs it away.

TAC EX 2 - The Insertion Tab.

On the insertion tab in, with his now badly packed lopsided Bergen the platoon move at a snail's pace. The weight seems fine for the first 15/20 minutes. I don't believe there is any science behind this, but Pte Crowbag does what every other soldier does in this situation: a weird hop shoulder shrug Bergen bounce.

This tactic removes the weight of the Bergen for approximately one 5th of a second. At first, the time between this move is every five minutes or so, but as time drags on, it sadly takes place every other step.

The 2nd evolution where the standards are dropped, is taking a knee. The change between first taking a knee and last taking a knee is somewhat drastic.
The moment your knee hits the floor the first time around, you're welcomed by a soft, supple, patch of virgin grass. The weight is not all that bad, your pride is high as you watch your arcs like a true warrior. Mid way through the insertion tab your choice of ground is somewhat lowered, you have two options available to you, sharp rocks and stinging nettles, naturally you take the rocks. The poorly packed Bergan weight is now a serious issue and you are changing knee position every five seconds whilst totally chinning off your arcs, scanning out barely a one meter radius, desperately searching for nothing more inviting than a place to lay down your knee. Eventually the previous minuscule fuckage you gave at the start of the tab has now completely diminished and your mind begins to wonder... Why the fuck am I here?

During the final stage of the tab the devil decides to join you and perches himself firmly on your shoulder (an unnecessary, extra weight). Dangerous thoughts such as, "If I just rolled my ankle, this would all be over" and "what is the minimum amount of pain I'd have to inflict to get off this shit?" begin to creep in, but Pte Crowbag soldiers on, too much of a pussy to chuck himself over a baby's head or suffer the humiliation of getting in the Jack wagon.

TAC EX 2 - the exercise

Pte Crowbag finally reaches the Harbour area where the bloke in front gestures a hand signal that he has never seen in his life. Rather than try and work it out he decides to instead play hand signal Chinese whispers and just chucks out what he thought he saw to the bloke behind. When the bloke gives Pte Crowbag a completely puzzled and concerned face wondering why he's doing the YMCA rather than the recognised hand signal, he just faces his front, in the hope that the problem will resolve itself.

After moving into the harbour and laying in the prone position looking through a Catterick woodblock for an enemy that they know aren't there, the Crows drop Bergen's and start building the harbour. Then they get time to square away their personal admin. This is when the constant "2IC move in" and "prepare to move" are shouted with 30 seconds' notice, meaning Crowbags can't really get anything done and they are in an even shitter state than they were when they first arrived.

Today Pte Crowbag is going to be in his first platoon attack. The excitement is building; visions of COD are dancing in his head and he can't wait to show just how much of an operator he is. Reality strikes within the first ten minutes… The day is long and includes dry run after bone dry run with constant section strong punishments for the same mongs making repeated mistakes. He secretly wishes for a Full Metal Jacket moment for said individuals but remembers back to the recruiting advert that made him join and how everyone should be respected. After a long ballache day its back to the harbour for a refreshing night's sleep. A pleasant kip may be on the cards if only this woodblock wasn't located in Bastogne in 1944 and was a hive of enemy activity all fucking night. However, for now, Pte Crowbag does not concern himself with such matters, he checks when he's on stag and gets snuggly in his green time machine.

BANG BANG BANG "contact" Pte Crowbag is not one to fuck about, he kicks himself out his doss bag and is all over it, squaring his mukkers kit away while they buddy buddy, it's a fucking dream team. He can envisage the Training Team watching him through NVG remarking on just how professional he is. It's his time to come to the fore, for the grey man becomes the Top Recruit. Tea and medals all round he thinks for a job well done as the full screws are happy with how it all went down. Stand down! Comes the welcomed shout and everyone is free to get their heads down again. Pte Crowbag looking at his Casio and sees that it's 01:12, he is on stag at 2am, and this is where that "jack on yourself" devil starts to plant its evil seeds. "It's not worth getting the dose bag out for that amount of time" "you'll be fine" it says as it convinces Pte Crowbag to just lay on his roll-matt. As the cold slowly kicks in, his wet kit drains his soul, clings to his skin and he lays on the floor shivering so much he looks like an extra from trainspotting on the dance floor. As potential hypothermia starts to take hold, he glances once more at his trusty Casio and see's it is now 01:18. Knowing how hard the last four frozen minutes have been would usually persuade any rational human to get their doss bag out, but the devil is still there… "worth it even less now" he chirps. Finally, Pte Crowbag grips himself, cracks the less emotional part of wet and dry routine and slips into his doss bag which feels like a NAAFI chick, heavy but warm.

"Crunch, crack, stumble, fucking thing, fucking place, oooft, where the fuck is he?" the sound a heartless man makes as he shuffles through the night, "Crowbag, Crowbag mate you're on stag". With a token "how cold is it?" he makes his way from his wank sack and really regrets his life choices as he slips his wet kit on. He follows the comms cord to a hand over which would make Madeleine McCann's parents look responsible, and he sits down. Handover complete and at 02:02 he is left staring into the dark only to check his watch every few minutes and tell his mukka how shit it is.

After four or five hours, it's now 02:18… Time to wake up the next bloke, he shuffles off the stag position and finds his relief, who is up in a flash and is putting on such a show of professionalism that Pte Crowbag is convinced there are some DS still watching them. Pte

Crowbag does not have another stag all night so hoping of no more contacts he sees the clear potential to even get a clean few hours of head down. After the handover, he grabs the comms cord and heads back to his basha. In Catterick they do not issue crows high tech NVG, it's a simple concept of holding your left arm out in front of your face with a flat palm trying not to lose an eye on a branch.

Once he gets to his basha he tries to slip into his bed space only to find someone there, "mate who's there" "it's Smudge, I've just been on!". Heartbreak. Pte Crowbag had followed the wrong way on the comms cord and now is in the wrong section. The jack on yourself devil has returned, "Pte Crowbag, if you follow the comms cord back around, it will take you ages to get back to your bed space, if you cut across the centre of the harbour you'll be there in no time."

Relying stupidly on the jack on yourself devil, Pte Crowbag makes his way through the darkness, round and round, stopping just the once for a little cry to himself. Eventually the poor bastard hits the golden comms cord… Success! Drenched and baltic he finds his kit and proceeds to get his head down.

By now, the exercise is slowly drawing to an end. But joy of all joy! The best is yet to come, the final platoon attack.

The scenario is a generic duty attend dawn attack on the enemy position, the enemy being played by REMFs and Biffs, (people I'd support using real ammo on) , it's freezing and only half the platoon fully understand what's about to happen.

Pte Crowbag is pumped and waiting in the harbour, on a knee in haribo formation (herring bone) waiting with the rest of the warriors as they are ready to move off. The advance to contact seems to last for ages but no Bergen's means it quite literally is a walk in the park. Then "bang bang bang - contact front" is yelled, Pte Crowbag fires his two rounds while taking a side step and is about to dive to the floor when he notices a large bed of stinging nettles, so a further few steps are taken, and then a couple more. Now he fully commits with a dive roll to get into the prone position.

The attack is a complete lick, but he keeps his head low and gets through it. With the enemy all perished and REORG in full swing, everyone's hopes are high that ENDEX will be called any minute. "BANG" - with that simple dropping of a pyrotechnic from a member of the directing staff he knows what's coming…MAN DOWN!!!

Causality is called, but Pte Crowbag has won the lottery… It is he who has been hit by the mortar round. He is placed on a stretcher cobbled together out of a basha and carried/dragged by four members of his section, the entire time being either on the floor or a clean one inch above it. A ray of sunshine pierces the grey Catterick sky, it shines on the cold wet ground and in the distance, he can see the Holy Grail that are the four tonners. Jobs a good 'un and his section is in the lead (for some reason this is now a competition) as they are about to hit the back of the transport its lights come on, and it starts to pull away "this can't be real life" he thinks to himself. The bastards! The fat useless REMFing driving bastards! There are nearly tears. He is broken. They have won.

Eventually, the world's longest CASEVAC comes to an end, ENDEX is called and everyone starts to de bomb. They make the required declarations and they are cleared off the back area. Off they trundle back to camp for the joy that is cleaning weapons.

This may or may not have happened

What follows is what can only be described as pure terror. While stripping their kit down one of the section finds a bandolier of 100 5.56 in his webbing, his declaration was false, will he go to the Glass House? Will the Section be hammered for lying to a Cpl when they did indeed have some live ammunition, blank ammunition, pyrotechnics or empty cases in their possession? WHAT TO DO!!!!?? As you can imagine this creates a great debate, CDRILS - be honest with the staff and pray for mercy, hide the ammo, amnesty box and hope to never get caught and everyone can keep their weekend.

The platoon put their heads together and after much deliberation they decided the best course of action was to ditch the ammo on another Platoon's floor. The ammo was put in another Platoon's drying room, was found by "cleaners", actually the blue rockets that walk around the block after the recruits have cleaned it who do nothing more than drinking brews and getting smashed by the staff. That platoon was absolutely melted for something they couldn't explain, then smashed some more for having the audacity to lie to their DS about how they had "no idea where it came from!". This was the week of their pass out.

The end.

In the dim and distant past there was a lanky internet troll with a speech impediment, I say troll, more just a guy with a mischievous nature, a scallywag if you will. This scallywag enjoyed the simple things in life, a refreshing corona, avoiding the gym, tax rebates and a spot of catfishing here and there.

On a chilly October evening, back in 2016, whilst snuggled in his dressing gown balls deep in the latest Avon catalogue wishing he had a girlfriend, he had the idea of checking out what local beauties were available for perusal on a popular dating app. It was then the epiphany happened, who buys Avon? Mostly girls.. So if I immerse myself as a female I'll better understand the female psyche and therefore sell more Avon? Great idea!

It was at this moment Isabella was conceived. After registering with a dating app (next logical step), he decided to transform into Isabella, a half Spanish photographer, who for no apparent reason, decided to relocate from sun drenched Spain to one mile outside of a dreary military village. This exotic young woman seemed to lust specifically after gullible, horny and naive Crowbags. Not only was Isabella tanned, toned and fit, she was also partial to a bit of casual anal. Before she knew it, her wish of wanting her arse split into two, ideally in a forestry block, was about to be granted…

Within an hour of registering on the app and a few messages back and forth a particularly gullible, horny and naive Crowbag dressed in full MTP arrived at the meet location. After taking multiple selfies to prove he was at said train station, he then received the following message "FYB doesn't approve of your PERSEC" followed by a winky face as the little minx was still in a flirty mood.

The cheeky little scamp lay there chuckling at his wit. Laying in his terry toweling Marks and Spencers Dressing Gown he could only imagine the sheer heartbreak our young Crowbag would have felt reading such a message, his love, his romance, his anal in the woods, had disappeared quicker than a clerk at the back of a ten miler.

Of course all of this was captured for posterity and shared online, for no reason other than to warn others of the dangers of online dating. In just a few moments, the hashtag #analinwoods was born, and with it a new sense of PERSEC within the military community. But blokes are blokes, mongs are mongs and most of all pests are pests. With his desire to increase the personal security of the Military satiated he made a tactical withdrawal to the comfort of his couch. Here he waited, waited and dreamed of catching a bigger fish. He knew he'd need to let some time pass, so in true debonair style, he cracked another ice-cold Corona and waited patiently for the fishing scene to relax its guard and let the water restock once more with nibbling little crowbags.

We leap forward to early August 2017, previous honey traps had failed on the favorite fishing sites due to the guys heightened awareness. Good he thought, they are learning. But in a true Darwinian response he realised he must adapt, improvise and survive if PERSEC was really to be taken to the next level. Despite casting far and wide there were no nibbles, the bait required must be more advanced, a lure if you will, and more importantly, this time the crows had to initiate first contact.

Utilising the Gold Silver and Bronze approach the plan was simple, an accomplice would create a fake profile of a damsel in distress, and using the fake profile to tug on those caring crowbag heartstrings said damsel innocently posts that she is "feeling awkward after attending a mess function with her boyfriend whilst two of her exes are there." And what ever should she do!? Moments later, a screenshot and status are posted to FYB. How very dare I!? This public outing of her predicament was more than her honour could withstand! TRIGGERED! My sexy accomplice then comments on the post asking, no, demanding that I should remove the post and all traces of herself from the page.

As expected, her comment attracted the attention of dozens of guys calling her a lizard/lizardo and if her morals were so loose she should just freestyle the function and enjoy the attention. .

One thing I have learnt since the conception of FYB, where there are lizards, there are snakes. And as it turns out FYB is a heavily infested reptilian zone. The trap was set, and like in Pulp Fiction where the spider catches a fly, the excitement was palpable. The twisted evil genius chuckled (with a lisp) as the friend requests came flooding in, messages of sincere support from guys just wanting to make sure she was ok. Such good blokes, sincere and honest in their intent and in no way putting down the ground work. From every angle they came, from guys in Catterick depot, to staff Sgts at battalion, everyone wanted a slice of that ass. The budding suitors used all their best lines, explaining how they train killers, they put wires in things that kill people, how they kick down doors for a living, all the lines that can help identify a true REMF.

But our tale doesn't end there, if anything this is both the highest and lowest point of FYB, it is the pinnacle of Catfish achievement! I mean to make a national newspaper, sublime, simply sublime. If the lion is the king of the jungle, it must be the King Cobra to head the reptile house. And no snake was ever as powerful as the hero who not only messages the lovely damsel in distress to offer advice, he then went on to send photos and messages describing exactly what he would do to her should he be picked as the lucky future ex number 4. Needless to say all this was posted online to offer a warning to other snakes hiding in the grass. Obviously he was tagged in the post where he was hammered in the comments, but, there's an unexpected twist. His grown up kids got tagged in… Then his Missus. Eh… Probably best to leave this one here…

I've sat and compared and contrasted the differences and similarities of what was advertised to be the experience of the average soldier ten years ago, and compared it to the 2018 advertisements of the Service you are being recruited for today. Things are different to say the least.

Army Adverts 2010

I went on YouTube and reviewed ads from 2010. Awesome, makes me want to join up again (if I can keep my beard but that's another story). Warry as fuck, lads running in slow motion off of helicopters, gunfire in the background with the phrase "for the excitement, for the action, for the adventure". Blokes clearing rooms with grenades, explosions, fast rope from a helicopter through the jungle, but plot twist! You land in a nightclub (probably Raoul's Rose Garden, but again that's a different story and we have neither time nor the antibiotics for that one!). All the way through the advert there's a common theme, "with pride, with honour, with professionalism" They are all this way. A mix of action, good times, and harsh reality. A CASEVAC into beach party showing the juxtaposition of the horror of war and the camaraderie that forges. All in all, it's the right mix of aggressive action and a social life with the blokes.

Army Adverts 2018

I was going to watch the 2018 adverts again, but having narrowly avoided eye cancer when I watched them previously I decided against it. To the credit of the marketing consultants who put them together, they have been burnt into my mind, I'd like to now tackle each one head on as I question their intentions.

"Will I be listened to in the army" - Short answer, no. I can only talk for myself here, obviously, but I did not expect when I joined the Army that I could brief people up while on the lower tier of the promotional hierarchy. The NLP message of the advert I actually found quite sinister. The downtrodden woman standing up to evil men. The woman in the ad says she was talked over in her previous jobs by men great, so they are targeting this recruitment advert at weak people. She later commissioned and now despite her extensive experience of making it through Sandhurst she now has the relevant experience required to lead a team. What it does fail to do however, is it fails to mention those men she now leads must pass a higher standard of fitness to their female counterparts, but hey ho, sometimes the patriarchy needs to suffer for its privilege.

"Keeping the faith" - This one annoyed me the most. Is it because I'm suffering from Islamophobia? Is it because I'm a militant atheist? No, I'm neither of those things. The reason it annoys me the most is this. Out of this year's inspiring offerings this is just a blatant outright lie. If you've not seen it I suggest you watch it once, for research purposes only. Word of warning though, try and locate some safety goggles first. Midway on a patrol one of the private soldiers takes off all his PPE, his shoes and socks, washes his feet and face in a stream and takes some personal time to pray. While this is going on someone tries to get in comms with the patrol and they cut him off. Who is this hoping to recruit? Surely it's setting them up for a fail when people are told they simply can't pray 5 times a day when the job does not allow it. If it was in camp I could live with it. But on exercise, it demonstrates a level of unprofessionalism that is just not acceptable in today's modern military.

Can I be gay in the army - Short answer, yes. More to the point no one cares, and if you join the RAF Reg people are actually quite surprised if you are straight. This one is annoying for a different reason, firstly if you're gay and are interested in joining the armed forces, then Google it. Google it and you will see that the MOD is voted one of the top LGBT employers in the country, Google it and you will see that the ban on homosexuals joining the Military was lifted in the mid 90's. Google it and you will see no one cares what your sexual persuasion is, we live in the 21st century and it really isn't that big of a deal. Aside from Google perhaps you could pop along to the local library and read one of the dozens of books written by soldiers about being gay and in the forces. To me, it's like "can I be ginger and be in the army?". It's not targeting the switched on gay community who want to join the Military, it's targeting gay mongs, and if there's one thing the army has enough of (for now) it's mongs. So I'm not sure what the best case scenario is for this advert, but I hope it reached its demographic of those ten blokes hanging out of the back of a Sailor at the duty attend, publicly funded London Pride event.

Joining the army – The joining process

As with any prospective employer, joining the military involves a series of interviews to make sure both you and it are compatible. The first and biggest step comes down to the individual and their desire to "Be the Best".

Army 2010

You've made that decision. You know what awaits you. You are ready to go to the valley of death in Sangin. You brace up. You open the door…
You walk into a career office. You see it is manned by soldiers, JNCOs mainly, someone who is currently serving and was sitting where you were in the not too distant past. They understand military job roles, depending on their own unit obviously, but would have worked with other units in most cases. They understand you, they understand what it takes to make that initial step through the door and the rush of emotions and questions in your head. They know the lifestyle and what is required of you as a soldier and the impact that has on family life. They advise on a fitness test they themselves have passed. They can fully explain what is required of you to get into shape to pass these tests and how to maintain it with limited resources. If you are lucky they may have had combat experience, but nearly all would have been on overseas exercises etc. On top of this they have "presence" you feel like you're starting your journey, as a civilian you look at the uniform and you have the aspiration to wear it and be like them. These people seemed to be examples of everything you've only seen on TV or on paper. They invest in you, the full gambit from booking you on Army

selection and pre para selection along with real examples of what I need to do to prepare myself mentally. The BARB test was only time you did anything on a computer. Personally, I decided to try joining the Parachute Regiment because I had a Para Reg recruiter. Pretty much he looked like an absolute warrior and not some fat mess like the others in that office.

Army 2018

What have we come to expect? Well, now, you go online and complete a form, a call centre is meant to call you back. Unsurprisingly this does not happen so you call it, you listen to the automated response and after trying every option available to speak to an actual human you finally get through. Unfortunately, they can't find your submission so you do it again over the phone. The person you are talking to is reading from a script, they get minimum wage and does not give two fucks if you go to RLC or RMP, as long as you join so they can hit their recruiting targets for their bonus at the end of the month. They take your details and pass you to a case officer. This case officer is a lizard of the highest order who is working there part time, the other half of her time she is studying for a BTEC in the theory of nail polish crossed with gender studies. She knows nothing more than what google could tell you or my grandad who did his national service in 1952. She is however, absolutely and completely qualified to book you on to stuff and send over generic documents for you to read. She is the type of person that will tell you you'll get issued everything you need, not because she wants to lie to you, she genuinely is that incompetent. And anyway, you just don't need to wear twisties on size 22 jeggings. At the time of writing this the computer systems had been so messed up, people have been waiting over a year to get through it. And that is before the epic that is the Captia Medical Screening where they will turn you away for that twisted sock you had 5 years ago. The fact you play competitive rugby 4 times a week with no issues is neither here nor there.

Joining the army – Phase 1(Basic Training)

Army 2010

I was aware of what was coming my way, well, as aware as I could have been. My expectations were managed insofar I knew my head would be shaved and I would be treated like a cunt for the first couple of weeks. The classic break everyone down to the same level and build them into a team, nothing I hadn't seen in the movies. The shock of joining the Army is always going to be there. However, the blow is less hard to take when well informed.

Army 2018

Nothing like I thought it was going to be. No one listened to my thoughts on how to get the best out of the recruits even though I should be respected for the precious unicorn I am. No time to pray during my eight milers no matter what time of the day it was or how much I was hanging out. No mobile phones on exercise so I can take selfies thinking I'm a door kicking heartbreaker when in reality I'm nothing more than material for FYB as I look like a right screamer. So what do I do? Obviously I DAOR after waiting two years to get to this stage. I go to the papers about the bullying culture of the Army and how they are culturally ingrained racists and misogynists. I get paid out over 120k because my legs hurt as the marching stride length isn't designed for short arses as having height standards is sexists so they removed them. Having weight standards for joining is sexists, so they removed them. (that unfortunately is true, don't believe me? Look it up)

When did you join? What are your thoughts? Please do not share them in any way shape or form, unless you have since joined the army and frequently crack your Bible, Quran or any other book of fiction out during combat - I'd love to hear from you, a tax rebate awaits.

Promotion courses often bring the best and worst out in people, they are taken from their comfort zone and are expected to perform whilst under the scrutiny of the Directing Staff. Nowhere is this scrutiny more prevalent than the model pit I mean we all need a graphical representation of the ground, on the ground. Because GPS and live feed is so last year. So who crowds round this microcosm of society? Let us discuss…

The DS watcher. You can spot these clowns a mile off, these are the cunts that are sat on their bergen for hours on end staring into space only to spring up and want to get all hands on when DS appear. Normally followed by a completely meaningless statement like "let's get a move on lads" or "let's get this cracked", coupled with the classic "we're in our own time now lads". Toilets. *Helpfulness rating 2/10*

Landscape artist. Easily on the spectrum of Military normality, this bloke LOVES models. He spends his nights and weekends building War Hammer Marines units kits which he says he sells on eBay. You know he doesn't, he knows he doesn't, but you keep up the charade as it means he'll stay in his room and not bother you when you all want to go out and get smashed without a societal recluse with the fashion sense of your average train spotter. He loves nothing more than spending the entire time on his knees spreading dirt and mud about shaping the ground, he wants to become one with the model, spends the entire time getting the rivers just right, he is an artist. *Helpfulness rating 8/10*

The moss collector. This guy, this is the guy is the hero we all need. He is solid, does exactly as he's asked he is reliable with menial tasks. All the shit that needs to magically happen in the background, he's on it. Filling water bottles, Making brews, sent out to pick up the right grass and he will leave no stone left unturned to get you exactly what you asked for. And in here lays the issue. You get what you asked for, not necessarily what you want.. You ask for some fern to demonstrate a forest block, so off he goes, 20 minutes later he comes back with a single leaf of fern, when asked why it took so long, it's because he was looking for one the same shade as the colour on the map. And for that reason, he's only a mid league player. *Helpfulness rating 5/10*

The got everything guy. Your actual mix of the universal soldier, Inspector Gadget and a Swiss Army Knife. If you have this guy then you've struck gold. He is the complete straight bloke and the guy you actually think you are, but really you're not. When the call goes out for model kits and you reluctantly hand over your little tin of mine tape and fuck all else. This guy breaks out a Tupperware tub which lurked in the bottom of his exquisitely packed bergan, you're eyes light up as he breaks out tape, talc, flags, ribbons of all the colours, even the occasional scale models of tanks and planes. What a star. *Helpfulness rating 10/10*

The section mong. This might be a difficult read for some of you. But the simple way to ID the section mong is to look out for who gets the shit ping. The section mong is the guy you would task with helping the moss collector (moss 2IC). Yet somehow he will be collecting stinging nettles, or getting lost, or going diffy for 45 mins and come back with 3 rocks and a

twig. There's no more to say really, If you can't spot the mong in your section, then it's you.
Helpfulness rating 3/10

The average bloke. This is the category most of us fall into. Not a super soldier, not a complete fucking screamer. He will collect moss if told to do so, and do it well, he will read the map and guide the artist, he will be the one helping to clear the area and putting the brews on for everyone else. If anything, he gives even less of a fuck when the DS are about just to prove that he's not out to impress anyone. Just wants to tick that box and get one day closer to deciding whether to click to freedom or tough it out to the pension trap.
Helpfulness rating 7/10

The jack bloke. What a cunt. We all know one and he's always landing on his feet. Did you hear about that guy that got a job as the driver for CDS, got his own penthouse flat in London with full subs and civvy clothes allowance?? It's him, back story is he answered a phone call in the Troop office and was meant to leave a message for another guy about that job. In true Jack bloke style he didn't pass on the message then applied for the now gapped position which needed an urgent fill. This guy is here for the ultimate box tick to climb that greasy pole of promotion as quickly as possible so he can take his foot even further off the gas than it currently is. This guy is by far the worst guy to have in your section, he is not a mong, he's not solid, he knows he is jacking but still does it, anything he is tasked to do has to be re done, he is slow, he has bouts of "crow mode" where he will just sit on his bergen and consider life, he sits chuntering about how little other blokes are doing while patiently waiting to even outshine the DS watcher. His only interjection is to tell you how he would have done it differently and complaining about the 2IC. He is to the section what a single mum is with 8 kids is to the welfare state. A fucking drain. *Helpfulness rating -1/10*

The 'signed off-switched off' guy. Not much to say about this guy apart from why? Why are people like him on these course? Is it retention? Is that why they're loaded? I mean nothing says retention more than a few weeks on Brecon as a sexy little treat to nail home that you've made the right decision to sign off. During the course he really doesn't give a fuck about what's going on. All he does is unhelpfully stand at the back giving lads shit about how useless they are. Never in the right place, never got the right kit, never on time. The sole reason for group beasting, but on a plus side makes a fantastic shit shield.
Helpfulness rating 3/10

We are sitting in company lines, it's raining, no one is happy about being in camp with nothing to do, apart from avoid shit details. The normal level of complaining is going on about everything from plugs being cut off our cooking equipment to catching a dose from the local harlots. The door opens, in walks the latest offering from Sandhurst. Standing in his issued power pose of authority in front of a room of lads fresh back from Afghan stands this green one pip wonder, jaw struck strongly against the ingrained hostility in the room…

Lads, I've jacked up a bit of something you'll all love. Picture the scene, free time off, latest high tech soft tail mountain bikes, free phys in the sun, bit of pissing up, who is interested!? Tell me more boss, tell me more! The package, you'll love it. Ten days' mountain biking in the Atlas mountains, it's additional leave so it won't come off your annual allowance, time out of camp having a swan on civvy bikes, what's not to like!? And lads, it's on duty as well so if you cream in you'll even get a PAX pay out. It's a fucking bargain is what it is lads, you'd be an idiot not to do it. Maybe it was the cleanliness of his uniform, maybe it was his greenness but we were eating out his hand like George Galloway pretending he was drinking milk. We were lapping that shit up, we were buzzing with it, (poor cunts, it's like we'd never been burnt before)

So, The big question on every one's minds. For ten days' mountain biking in Morocco, what is it going to cost us? £195, that's it, and the rest covered by company funds, fucking sold. He had us, he had us at hello. Ten days thinking we're sponsored Red Bull racers for the price of a decent weekend on the lash? I'm so excited as I type this I think I'd sign up for it again!

But then through the fog of my deliria, my memories return, bad memories, sad memories. Time has passed and money has been paid, we are now two weeks out before AT starts, everyone has paid up, everything is squared.

POW!! from outa nowhere! Lads, looks like we can't get the correct insurance so everyone must get their own... No issue boss it's only a tenner, still totally worth it.

CRUNCH!! The hits keep a coming. Lads, I've spoken to the RAO and there was a bit of confusion over if this would be taken out of leave or not. Turns out we were wrong and it will come off your allowance. We? Fucking we!? There was no we. You said it was a buckshee fortnight in Morocco, there was no mention of taking our own leave for 2 weeks. Yeah sorry about that then lads, but in that case, here's a bit of good news then! It's only a week now so you've saved a bit of your own time there (pops smoke, moonwalks out of room before he's lynched).

OOOFT!! Turns out the trip has not be authorised to go off mainland Europe by some absolute screamer based in Andover. Back to the drawing board lads, it's no drama though, we're just going to have to look at other locations, Spain or Italy is still an option, somewhere we have a British military footprint, easier to arrange that way. Fair enough Boss, less traveling time and the food will probably be better (still trying to see the positives)

WHAMMY!! Lads, its' now too late to organise funding for T&S so we'd need to pick that up ourselves, not that it really matters as there are no flights available for us and no accommodation for a group this big. But we're still going biking so you're still quids in! But we're going to have to stay in the UK, basically we will be mountain biking in Brecon. Off he trots thinking he's done us all a solid favour. Absolute shocked faces in the room, it's like we've just been told that the 7 RHA are actually a real Para unit.

CRASH!! Lads, as we are now doing it in the UK it means we've had to change provider. What does that mean Boss? Basically, the company organising the mountain bikes has not come through so we are now in Brecon for a week with no bikes, so perhaps a bit of hill walking? I'm not going to lie, at this point we knew what was coming...

SHAZAM!! Since we are hill walking in Brecon, and the Boss is on selection maybe we can use this as a bit of map reading and do a little bit of NAV, to time obviously, and since we are in the Reg and not hats we might as well take 35lb + water.

In summary, we were suckered in, lied to and ended up paying £195 to get smashed on the hills. Bargain!

Army personnel will always complain, always. And one of the biggest causes for dissatisfaction in the Army is the pay. Whether it be a COs Big Breakfast, or the Continuous attitude survey, pay will always feature as a negative point.

But let us look at those figures, and I mean really honestly look.

The salary I'm using for this breakdown is based on a senior Tom / level 7 private soldier on about £26k a year, give or take.

You could always go down the route of hours worked and split it from there. As the Army always likes to tell you, you are always on duty (apart from when you're not for insurance and pay out purposes but that's a whole different story!). So, doing some simple maths, that would allow us to see what the hourly rate is. 26k divided by 365 days gives you £71.23 a day. £71.23 divided by 24 hours means that you're earning around £2.96 per hour. And remember the minimum wage for an adult in the UK is £7.83, age dependent.

So, is the Army really such a badly paid job? I'm going to review my average week in work and see how much I actually earn an hour. Remember this is based on a buckshee Tom in the Reg, zero responsibility and zero fucks to be had.

Taking a look at an average week in an average Unit.

Monday. As with all good units Monday is a 2pm start. Rock up in PT kit for a nominal role by the Sgt Maj, anyone in trouble over the weekend? No? good. Off you go to do some PT. A nice little 5 miler to start the week easy. Get in, have a shower, slip into uniform and back to company lines for 3:30pm basically to be told to look out for detail later. Keep an eye on WhatsApp, just remember not to call anyone mate.

Actual hours worked, 1 hour 30mins, you could argue it was 2 and a half hours but the last hour doesn't really count as this was spent sat in office drinking brews chatting about weekend.

Tuesday. Shock horror, today is a full day. PT at 8am which lasts for an hour then back into the company lines for 10am. You then hard target around camp trying to avoid dickings as best as you can. Pro tip. Try the skive to survive method and carry some paperwork from one building to another and before you know it it's 12 o'clock and you head off for lunch. Back into the office for 2pm and spend the next three hours waiting for detail. Actual hours worked, three.

Wednesday. Standard start of getting down to the gym for 8am, do a circuit, back to the office for 10am and discuss what you can square away for a sports afternoon without it being too much of a piss take the chain of command might notice. You manage to drag this out to lunchtime, again 12 till 2pm. Turn up at the sports field for 2 (unless you're a Pad but that is a separate issue) then play football for the afternoon. Hours worked, zero.

Thursday. The usual routine of turning up at the gym for 8am, back at lines for 10am. The Sgt takes a nominal to make sure no one is dead or hiding in a bin somewhere and you get sent to your room for personal admin. Personal admin, what a great term. This is the where you take your field kit out, check it for serviceability, report any defects and make sure your uniform is up to the standard required... Who am I kidding! This is where you have a wank, play call of duty, and have a brew. This "admin" continues into lunch time and then back down lines for 2pm. You get called up the office to be told you have a tab in the morning so you need to prep for it. You then spend a few hours doing some minor shit like go help clothing stores for couple of hours or do the mail run for the Sgt Maj or some other bone task. Time rolls on and you manage to cut away about half 3. Hours worked, three.

Friday. It's dark, It's early, you think to yourself, why can't this have been done yesterday afternoon? The reason for your grumble is an 8 o'clock start for a tab doesn't sound too bad. But in reality... You're all set with your 35lb plus water as you are switched on and did that yesterday between wanks. But an 8 o'clock start means a 6 o'clock alarm, you get up, you tape your feet if you need to, make sure your socks and boots are right and off to breakfast as you really need that SODEXO goodness in you pre tab. Turn up at 0700 at the armoury ready for the complete farce that is drawing weapons, the duty armourer is late, they issued the wrong weapon now they have to muster, all stress you don't need this early on a Friday morning. Turn up at lines, nominal is called and away you go. Tab complete, we stretch off, clean our already clean weapons till noon and get cut away. Total hours worked, three.

So all in all the average week contained about 11 hours of what you could call "work" over the course of a month that's a grand total of 44 hours. At £2166 a month. That's £50 an hour. To put that in to real terms a new GP will earn £31.25 an hour, so not bad really, and the amount of time you spend in the gym during the day means you don't have to during the evening, unless you're on OP Massive of course.

Yeah we can discuss ops, and dangers of the job, short notice pings and working weekends etc. But I think most of us can't really chunter how much we banked while spending more time on porn hub than the ranges.

Show parade, what is their point, really? A quick explanation of a show parade to a civilian would go something along the lines of; you have been found guilty of some minor infraction and your punishment is to get your uniform, and your person, checked out to make sure everything is in order. But it's more than that really, as you can be expected to be in different bits of uniform at different times, for example you may need to be in Barrack Dress at 1600, but then in MTP at 1630, barely enough time to get from the guardroom, to the accommodation then back to the guardroom. And that's the point. To put it simply, it's a fuck about designed to waste your time. But if you spend some time thinking about it, it's a weird, if not slightly homoerotic, ritual used only to confirm power over an individual.

I understand depot ones. Phase one trainee, you're a bit of a wide boy and think you can buck the system as it's just a bit of ironing. Well, a few runs back and forth to the Platoon Office in various states of dress, which means you need to meticulously iron every bit again before you stow it away in your locker will soon teach you the errors of your ways. Show Parades in Depot is just one of those things, a weapon in the DS arsenal used to correct bad admin,.I always felt I'd rather take a beasting and keep my evenings clear than get fucked about all night. You could argue that it worked as a fairly good deterrent. Thing is these continue into Battalion. I for one was lucky enough in my time in battalion to never get a show parade, a couple of promotion bans sure, but never a show parade. I went full retard when I decided to drop a bollock.

The thing I always found weird about battalion show parades; is just the sheer awkwardness and pointlessness of it all. You turn up late, through no fault of your own, you've read part one orders but missed a WhatsApp chat as your phone is out of data. This led you to be 10 minutes late to a detail. You followed the last lawful order you were given but somehow this is your fault. Punishment? Show parade. Fucking brilliant, that's a night wasted. So, you turn up 5 minutes ahead of time outside the block stood to attention waiting on the duty officer to come along. And here you are… You are having a junior officer, who you more than likely know quite well, look over you like a piece of meat. Both of you trying not to laugh at the ridiculousness of it all. The charade element for me is the obvious fact. If they wanted to fail someone, they could fail them, no matter how squared someone is you could find something for a reshow. This leads me to believe if you put in a solid amount of effort and fail you may have to consider, am I just a shit cunt?

I'm going to start this with a gen dit, a full screw of mine in depot, we'll call them Smudge, and to be honest, from depot to Battalion they were someone I admired for their devotion to soldiering. But like every Jeckle, he had a Hyde, he was a fucking cunt of DS. I mean a proper shit cunt (see encyclopedia for full definition). He knew how to "correctively train" depot blokes, let's leave it at that. In the first few weeks when we had show parade in the block lines there was about 30-40 Joes lined up in his corridor. He came out at 10pm and spoke about CDRILS and said if anyone had anything they could get picked up for, step forward. If they admit it he won't pick them up for it. About six blokes stepped forward. He then said "you six, reshow, everyone else pass." You had to admire this. Psychological warfare right there. You knew that if you were on show parade again, and he asked the same question, this time you didn't step forward yet you were still picked up you'd get the thrashing of your life. The fear was real.

On that note, there always seemed to be three distinct categories of blokes when it came to kit. These blokes are ona sliding spectrum of how they handled show parade, these guys include:

- Squared blokes, these are the guys who somehow only ever get put on when its platoon strength, never an individual dicking,
- Middle of the road, says it all, the "once in a while" the fucked up guys.
- The Platoon Mongs, the completely dedicated full time every night guys, it's part of their routine, the type of blokes that still had three more nights to pass after they failed that nights.

The squared blokes would be stood down at 6 or 7pm square their kit for that night, get their kit squared for the morning, call home for a catch up with their mrs, do a bit of "best book" and pass that night with flying colours.

The middle guys are similar, but they may look at some kit and think "it will do", their kit is done to the minimum standard for the next day, and that phone call home is replaced with two hours of looking at FYB.

The platoon mongs, these guys are just resigned to failing show parade one minute after being stood down, their kit in a pile at the bottom of their locker, they fuck off to the NAAFI or another sections room to shoot the shit. Show parade will not cross their minds till around 2140 for a 2200 showparade. And while the squared and middle of the road blokes are dressed and polishing the back of their cap badge, these mongs are running around trying to borrow a clean smock.

The only thing to compound this misery is the weather. You form up and make your way to the guardroom as a platoon, the rain is pissing sideways and the kit which was immaculate a few moments ago now looks as if they it's been in the field a week. Show parades, shit 'em.

There are very many differences between the way you get treated as a Married soldier and a Single soldier, from allowances to time off, but today we're going to head off into the world of "fiction".

This is the story of the 22 year old Cpl Smith. He is a member of the elite Royal Electrical Mechanical Engineers and has been serving for 4 years. A side note to any Yanks reading this or those that are not familiar with REME, they are tier one babysitting service, their crest is a pony, and every now and then they fix stuff.

Cpl Smith came to a crossroads just after leaving basic training, does he stay with his lizard or not? Does he commit to this significant other from back home or should he break up with her to be free to make love to the most beautiful women in the world from exotic locations such as Chippenham, Catterick and Colchester? If he is really lucky, he might even get the chance to roll the AIDS dice in Kenya. Young Smudge thought long and hard about his options and despite taking his emotions out and doing a full cost benefit analysis, he decided the way to have head rule over heart would be to flick a coin. These are the parallel stories of both sides of that coin.

Accommodation at Battalion.

Single.
On showing up at battalion Smudge was issued a key to a room that a mute, deaf and blind refugee would chin off. This room is the size of a large cupboard. If he stretched his arms out he could touch both sides of the wall at the same time. There is sink for washing, shaving and having a pee into. There are 2 electrical sockets, both under the bed that is bolted to the floor, and of course he can not use an extension cord to send power to a more convenient place, such as the desk fixed to the wall, as this would be against the QMs directive and would result in him getting a minor sanction against him. He opens one of the 2 fitted wardrobes and muses to himself about how he's going to get his barrack dress, field kit, civilian kit and still fit the TV he'll have to hide should the QMs want to do block inspection for a TV without a License. It is then he sees the mattress for his bed. This 3 inch rubber bit of pustulating infection source has seen more orgasm's than a pornhub search bar. He weeps. He lives on a floor with 24 other guys. Some of these guys are actually normal people, might drink the occasional pint of piss, but over all normal. Some have been in two months longer than he has and think they own the place, some have been in four or five years and are sound, some are functioning alcoholics who love nothing more than beasting the new bloke for a lift to a kebab shop at 3am. He quickly settles into the routine of night after night being called to act as the midnight taxi, getting briefed up what he's doing wrong, mostly based on the fact he joined later than other guys due to his parents jacking on him and not giving birth to him sooner. He noticed that in this microcosm of society it seemed to be the fatter, biff bods seem to do the most briefing. And for this 5* accommodation he would pay £78, a bargain I'm sure you would agree.

Married.

On showing up at battalion Smudge is issued a key to a three-bedroom house. Fantastic he thinks, thank you Army! Only thing is, it seems like it was built during the cold war and yet somehow they managed to decorated in a style reminiscent of the 1940s. Retro cool. Complete with magnolia woodchip wallpaper and holes filled with toothpaste which have been painted over in a gloss paint that makes them even more obvious than if the previous occupier had just left the picture hooks in. It smells slightly of piss and 3 day old shitty nappies, the taps spit out brown water and damp mould fills the air. The furniture looks like the British heart foundation have binned it and looks like it wouldn't pass modern fire standards. Luckily the house is made completely out of asbestos so that's something at least. The "march in" happens and a nice guy from Carillion shows him round (not taking his shoes off and tramping mud into the cream carpets which he will later charge him to get cleaned). Walk round complete he gets him to sign all the paperwork and promises they will not be charged for anything that they do not damage as he's noted all the bumps and scrapes where previous pets have eaten part of the skirting board, and even though they don't own a dog, that is also something they will get charged for when they leave. Reassurances are made about how any outstanding repairs will be remedied within a fortnight. This is said in the same tone as telling a child everything will be ok after a doctor just told you you've got two weeks to live. The child, like you, knows the person is lying, but it's easier on everyone to play along and hope for the best.

Single.

A Cpl now and having served four years or so, Smudge is a fine JNCO, he is capable in every aspect of his job, He is well respected and well liked, and trusted by seniors to mentor the new blokes as they come in. His two Herrick's, and various other overseas deployments under his belt which has allowed him to save for a house meaning he will soon be on the property ladder. He has managed to win at the IED roulette game in Afghan, swerve the CDT in Belize and avoided getting a local hippocrocapig (see encyclopedia for full definition) pregnant. He is flying. He has recently been put in charge of the armory. He is accountable to both military and civilian law with multimillion pound weapon systems by day, but at night he is not to be trusted with a toaster or microwave, this perfectly capable human being is told with a straight face that the kitchen area in the accommodation is not to be used for cooking as it's a "food preparation area" and not a kitchen. He can brush aside the constant additional last minute weekend duties because other blokes have kids and as a single man he doesn't need his weekends. This just allows him to save more money for his deposit. What he can't cope with is that since he can't cook for himself and the scoffhouse is below the standard required of prison food, he eats shite every night, will it be Dominos, Rollovers or Maccy D's? Being in the armoury and the constant EC inspections, snap inspections, CO inspections, OC inspections he is ground down. He starts jacking on PT and over the course of a year is now a fat, lazy, resentful armourer. Passion for his job has gone. Why? Treat a man like a child, they will act like one. He signs off at the first opportunity.

Married.

A Cpl now and having served four years or so, Smudge is a fine JNCO, he is capable in every aspect of his job, He is well respected and well liked, and trusted by seniors to mentor the new blokes as they come in. Being married he has never deployed, his wife can't cope with him being away and the Welfare SNCO has came through every time. He is flying. He has recently been put in charge of the armory. He is accountable to both military and civilian law with multimillion pound weapon systems. Being in the armoury and the constant EC inspections, snap inspections, CO inspections, OC inspections he quickly realises that he can't possibly manage to get home to pick the kids up on time so formulates a plan using the flexible working time directive to share the work out among the rest of his team. His Sgt keen to show how with the new modern age Army he is enthusiastically agrees that our man shouldn't have to shoulder the responsibility of his role on his own, because what's a couple of working weekends to the singlies anyway, it's not like they do anything at the weekends anyway. This allows him to strike that magical work life balance, maintain a high level of fitness and still get away early. The dream. Passion for his job is at an all time high as he delegates responsibility to his peers, smashes his courses and is picked up as a Sgt at the first time of asking.

From the very beginnings of your service career there will always be a single constant. And that constant is disappointment. Nowhere is this disappointment more obvious than with military transport From day one week one you will have had to endure a wide array of movements. Whether it be in training with 4 tonners, busses or the mythical Helo insert that never arrives. Or when you're in battalion where you spend days upon days of your life waiting on flights. When it comes to the dog of war what makes the teeth of troops bite and the tail of the logistics follow on? Is it an elite bunch of operators? No, it's the Retards Last Chance (RLC) and the failed fast jet pilots (RAF Movers)

UK exercise

Certain things in the Army are always guaranteed, for example. The end of exercise is called, debomb, and off back to camp for a shower and food. Shocker, no coach or Mann truck turns up. you wait, and wait, and wait some more. Time goes by, transport eventually turns up. Hurrah! Now for a real life example of how the Army can twist the knife, transport turns up. But there is only enough space for three quarters of the people there. We are left with 2 options, walk back, or wait some more. We walk. A mere 4 miles back to the accommodation. Naturally by the time we get back the water is cold and the food is gone. But it's a bit of free phys, so, you know, every cloud. In full fairness to the Boss he loaded as many lads on as he could, people even gave up seats so they could put others kit on and walked back as well.   Take the transport troops tardiness the other way, in the history of the military has there ever been a time where transport is late to get you on your way to Otterburn or Brecon? Simple answer is no, no it has not.

Overseas exercise

Heading out to Cyprus for a two-week confirmation exercise. You have a flight at 1400 from Brize Norton to Cyprus. You're coming up from Bulford so it's just under an hour and a half drive. The check in is at 1100 as you have weapons to get loaded, three hours before take off seems fair. Naturally the head shed doesn't see any point in taking any chances so you they call an 8 o'clock start. As sods law dictates there's no traffic and you get there around half nine, obviously you're too early to check in so you need to wait. Due to the need for a weapons sentry you can't even get sorted with brews. Your mind wanders to the three options that will come to the fore.

1. You will instantly be told the flight is delayed due to some erroneous reason. There's a chance the plane is actually bust but there's also a fair chance the pilot didn't have his eggs in his favourite silver egg holder that morning so he's thrown a strop and is currently sulking waiting on a blow job from the cabin crew to make him feel like a real pilot rather than the flying taxi driver he actually is.
2. You will check in at the expected time, get through security and enter the waiting lounge. You're a vet at this shit and you know what's coming so you make your way straight to the kids play area, stretch out and wait on the news that the flight has

been delayed due to the pilot overhearing someone describe him as nothing more than a flying taxi driver. You look around playing smash or pass at the various attached ranks, Medics, usually quite fit but usually engaged before they leave basic training to some three times divorced full screw. Chefs, never trust a skinny chef, these look trustworthy. Admin clerks, bitter and repressed individuals who realise they are only tolerated due to the fact no one want to work with the RAO. They are looking for a reason to fuck your pay up, best avoided. RLC Mover, you're not even convinced they're human. Next comes the announcement the flight is cancelled and you settle in for the long haul. The shop isn't open and the coffee machine only takes the old style 50p, not that it matters as it only has powdered mushroom soup in it. You sleep.

3. Flight will leave more or less on time.

You know it'll be option 2 so you roll over, ask yourself why and sneakily eat the whole packet of tangtastic you've secreted in your pocket. Time passes and you're given a shake. Call forward has happened and the order of loading is Senior Officers, Officers, SNCO, Cannon Fodder. You muse that it'll make far more practical sense to load the lads first, move everyone straight to the back of the plane and fill up from there. That doesn't happen as everyone has been playing the mental smash or pass and decied to go ugly early with the shaved gorilla that is the mover and try to sit with her/it.

After the total cluster fuck your flight is good to go, you're in your seat, the flight attendants are not like anything you'd see on a BA flight never mind an Emirates one. You might get one smash out of a crew of passes but the rest are passed over 40 year old Cpls wearing beige flight suits that are too tight for them and they just look like marshmallows tied in string.

Word	Meaning
Accommodation	A living area worse than most jails, where 50 men and all their equipment are made to live. The three females present on the exercise will have one of these blocks entirely to themselves.
Army recruitment	A joke we all fell for
Bine	Cigarette. Bines serve three major functions within the military: To give the blokes on punishment duties fag ends to pick up, to be bought cheaply in foreign countries and sold back in the UK at a profit and to be scrounged for on exercise by a smoker fails to bring any out with him.
Blanket Punishment	A commonly employed military technique that is in breach of the Geneva Convention. Involves an entire section or platoon being denied privileges for something that one bloke did
Blue rocket.	
Brecon point	
Buckshee	It's "free" or additional to surplus, not all buckshees are equal however, if you meet a man with three combi tools he is not to be trusted.
Cam	(Camouflage) Net - A large patch of material that can be spread over several vehicles or structures, instantly creating a bulletproof shield of invisibility that disguises you from the enemy, even when the net is a different colour from the environment.
CDT	Compulsory Drugs Test. An on the spot test issued by the Army to ensure that drug taking soldiers can be identified and then kept in the Army because severe retention issues prevents them from being kicked out.
CDT	Compulsory drug test, never understood blokes failing a drug test, Been to my fair share, and the way they are run, for me ar completely bizarre. I assume their goal is to catch as many blokes as possible
Chef	A job role that was looked down upon for decades, until civilian contractors such as Sodexo took over military feeding, at which point all military personnel began to miss them terribly.
Comms	An entire platoon of highly trained blokes, who work night and day to establish essential radio and data communications which then fails to work and somebody is nominated to walk or run around delivering messages like a less effective carrier pigeon.
Corporal	The actual most important rank in the Army. Consists mainly of people who possess enough experience and skill to be an asset to the unit and yet are still junior enough to spend their time teaching and managing their soldiers. Sometimes found in training establishments calling people "Crowbags" and dishing out blanket punishments.

Craphat	also known as screamer, hat, Horaldo or Harry. A term used by paratroopers to describe every other regiment. As a side note, there are four parachute regiment battalions, the above terms can also be used by craphats who are in denial such as members of 7 RHA.
Diffy	When you're missing a bit of kit, or one of the blokes is missing on the piss. They are diffy, "where is Smudge" "He went Diffy with that fat lizard in revs"
Dits	Loosely translated as "story", dits are a detailed and often exaggerated re-telling of an event of bravery and hardship. Usually told in the Naafi by a bloke who has never been on tour or seen combat.
Dossbag	A piece of miltary sleeping equipment also known as a gonksack or green time machine or simply bomb. For example, I got into my green time machine for seven hours head down and was on stag three minutes later.
Fijian	One of the most highly represented Commonwealth soldiers in the British Army. They spend their time playing Rugby, drinking grog and inflicting severe violence.
Garages	A place where the Battalion or Squadron vehicles are stored. During the working day contains 70% of all available manpower, who will be engaged in the important task of standing around pretending to know what they are doing.
Gay	Pronounced "Gayyyyyy" an adjective not to be confused with a person's sexual preferences, for example a member of the navy. Most appropriately used to describe someone who willingly chooses to spend time with their girlfriend / Wife instead of drinking with the blokes.
Gen	The most overused word in the military, short for "genuine" or "genuinely". Can be used at the start, middle or end of a sentence to add authority to what you're saying. "Gen need to be at the armoury" or "Mate we are standing down at 2pm gen"
Good bloke	ironically, not a term of endearment but the best way to describe a shit cunt, a guy who tells the boss you're in your room when you've told him you've got an emergency dental.
Gopping	Blokes, chick, food, PT - Anything can be gopping. "Scoff is gopping" "that lizard is gopping" Battle PT is gopping.
Guard Duty	The act of providing 24 hour manning on a camp or location to provide help in an emergency, such as an intoxicated soldier losing his room key.
Gurkha	Legendarily ferocious soldiers who have served in the British Army for centuries after we realized we could not defeat them in battle. Comes with a choice of three different surnames.
Harbour	Any area safe from enemy activity, where soldiers are supposed to sleep, eat and rest. Attempting to sleep, eat or rest will result in having blank rounds fired in your direction and being made to move to an identical looking woodblock 500m up the track.
In Your Own Time	An expression used to imply that a soldier has a choice of whether he wishes to finish work for the day or to continue a completely boring and unnecessary job. Said soldier will be punished if he does not complete the job.

Infantry

The bayonet thrusting, door kicking, grenade throwing, widow making frontline combat soldier. Spends his time looking down on all non-Infantry soldiers and secretly resenting that they do a less exhausting job, get treated like adults, get promoted quicker and develop transferable skills for when they leave the Army.

Jack

Someone with the reliability of a split condom

Lance Corporal

An ambitious and talented person who is caught between proving himself worthy of the new responsibility he has been given and his mates one rank lower than him, who refuse to follow his orders and constantly tell him "You've changed" when he tries to make them work.

Lizard

every woman you will ever come across throughout your life. Also called Lizuardo, three genders

MATTS

A complete training program that details all essential aspects of being a soldier. Covers fitness, first aid, mine clearance, weapon handling, casualty evacuation etc. Is generally taught to you in less than 15 minutes by a newly promoted Corporal who last revised these things when he was in depot 7 years ago.

Medic

An individual who can theoretically be the difference between life and death on the battlefield, but in reality hands out ibuprofen and hay-fever tablets. Is sometimes an attractive female, though generally not as attractive as QARANC nurses.

Nails

A bloke known for his fighting capabilities, willing to fight anyone and everyone

Non-Tac

Short for 'non-tactical' when on exercise in a job role that is non-enemy facing and so do not need to observe noise or light discipline. This will last for approximately twelve hours, at which point somebody of rank will come to observe the exercise and you are then made to dig a trench worthy of the Western Front in 1916.

Officer

An individual trained to be a leader and manager in the Military. Often has a University degree, a private school accent, a clean driving license, a steady relationship and other things that ordinary soldiers are incapable of achieving.

Part One Orders

(AKA Detail) A comprehensive list that covers every soldier in the company or squadron and what tasks, courses and appointments they have to achieve today. Has become completely irrelevant since the invention of WhatsApp groups.

Pest

PFA

A basic fitness assessment designed to test a soldiers ability to run 2.4KM in a short period of time. Often cited as being unrealistic, unimportant and not relevant to warfare by people who cannot pass it.

Private

A generally confused, unhappy individual who does not understand the task he has been given or why he is doing it. Often tells his civilian friends that he is a highly trained killing machine, even though he spends most of his time picking up cigarette ends and sweeping floors.

Provo

A person responsible for ensuring discipline within a military camp. Often seen carrying a pace stick, issuing parking tickets, looking for excuses to AGAI the newest bloke in battalion and denying that they were bullied in school.

PTI	Physical training instructor, to accomplish this position, you need to pass an intensive course and agree to use hair products and skinny jeans exclusively.
Ranges	A place where soldiers can perfect the essential skill of accurate shooting in order to kill the enemy by spending six hours sat in the rain, firing 30 rounds through a rifle that has not been zeroed and then a further two hours cleaning all weapons, including the ones that haven't been fired.
Rations	A box containing food for 24 hours, perfectly formulated to keep a soldier fighting fit on the battlefield and provide all necessary nutrients. Is promptly not eaten by said soldier, who chooses instead to live on noodles, haribo, hotdogs and cigarettes.
RMP	"Monkeys" Basically there to crush any morale, never solved a crime, Has the same legal powers of arrest as postman Pat's black and white cat.
Robogen or Eyebrows	Basically putting a guarantee on what your saying to be true. For example "mate we are standing down at 2pm Eyebrows" at 2:01pm any soldier who heard the phase said is legally entitled to shave the offender / Liars / Man of no integrity eyebrows off. True example of this; South African para reg bloke on a jumping exercise in Northern england, Sitting around on camp cotts shooting the shit over scoff. Horror bags, with a orange club bar. Said SA tucked into this new found treat and said.. Orange clubs are nice, never had one. Quick as anything his mortor mukka replied "robogen you've never had one " ... "robogen never had one" "but you just had one" from that word to looking like robocop was max 3mins
SA80	
Shaving Chit	A highly desirable piece of paper that allows a soldier to be made exempt from the daily routine of shaving. Is given out under very extreme circumstances such as severe facial swelling, contagious skin diseases or being a Commonwealth soldier.
Social hand grenade	A good soldier, Good in the field, never late, reliable, but get 2 pints on him and he tries to take on half of a Weatherspoon's with the ancient fighting technic of "wind milling" he can't be brought back from the edge once he is there
Solid	Not always a mong, but someone that needs three examples and five attempts at anything, whether it's map reading or simply filling a water bottle. Did you hear about the guy that....That guy is solid.
Sports Afternoon	A time honoured tradition that dates back decades, where all soldiers are excused from working on a Wednesday afternoon to pursue their sporting interests such as playing X-Box and masturbating in their rooms.
Stag / guard	
Stand by	Everyone's least favourite phrase, can be used as a warning for future punishments. Used normally in conjunction with profanity for maximum effect. Eg 'you fucking lot can stand the fuck by, you fucking cunts'
Stand down	Everyone's favourite phrase, this is when the 26 year old corporal is told he's allowed to drive home.
Straight bloke	again, this term is not to be used to describe one's sexuality, instead refers to the kind of bloke that doesn't bang out a danger wank at 3am in the guard room, stagging on the phone.
Switched on	A bloke who has his shit together, knows his job well and can be relied on.The opposite of "solid" bloke.

TAB	An acronym for Tactical Advance to Battle, in which soldiers rapidly march in full kit over a number of miles for the purpose of irreparably damaging their back and knees.
Tracksuit soldier	An individual with an exceptional talent for a sport, usually football, rugby or boxing who is never seen in military uniform or holding a rifle but somehow still gets promoted.
Training Wing	A place that tracks all qualifications held by the soldiers in a unit and then promptly loses all paperwork related to it.
UBAC	A tight-fitting, long sleeved shirt, more suitable for the field than camp that either shows off your impressive chest and biceps or clings to your ample belly and flabby chest, depending on your physique.
Virtus	The result of millions of pounds spent in government and military research that has created a fairly decent helmet and absolutely nothing else.
Warm Kit	Items of kit issued to soldiers to prevent them from being cold and suffering non-freezing cold injuries. Will be promptly replaced by civilian clothing that actually accomplishes this.
Welfare	A team devoted to assisting soldiers with all aspects of their personal lives, that is primarily used by the soldiers wife to complain when he is made to do his job.
Wet Kit	Significantly better than military issue Warm Kit in that it actually does accomplish its primary aim of keeping the soldier from getting wet. Unfortunately you are unable to wear it without having your masculinity, sexuality and ability as a soldier aggressively and sometimes violently questioned.

Printed in Great Britain
by Amazon